IN PURSUIT
OF TH
LAST

Front Cover - A2 Class 60528 *Tudor Minstrel* stands alongside A3 60052 *Prince Palatine* at Dundee (Tay Bridge) depot. (and page 93)

Inside Front Cover - A4 Class 60026 *Miles Beevor* sets out from Doncaster with the down 'White Rose'. Nov '61.

Inside Back Cover - The inevitable sad end to an A4 as 60015 *Quicksilver* is towed to Doncaster works for cutting up in May 1963.

IN PURSUIT OF THE LAST PACIFICS

BRIAN LISTER

Contents

Dedicated to my wife who like many other wives of the 'trainspotting' fraternity has patiently endured my obsessive, single-minded, selfish, 'no-thought-for-what-I-want-to-do', attitude whenever my enthusiasm for trains has gained the upper hand and, temporarily at any rate, has illogically rearranged the domestic order of priorities.

Published 1999 by RailArt Publications
Holme House
Oakworth
Keighley
West Yorkshire
BD22 0QY

ISBN 0-9536150-0-6

Printed in England by Amadeus Press Ltd. Huddersfield

Introduction

Of all the locomotive types built for Britain's railways throughout the entire period of steam traction, none have evoked quite the same passion as the 4-6-2s, commonly known as pacifics. These engines, from various origins and in widely differing designs and styles epitomised the ultimate form of motive power for the heavy express passenger trains over the last half century of steam operation.

In the mid 1950s, the post war hey-day of pacific steam activity, no one ever doubted that sooner or later, diesel and electric power would replace steam traction over the railway network. After all, prototype locomotives had already been on extensive trials. As early as 1948, the twin LMS diesel electric locomotives 10,000 and 10,001 were hauling west coast main line expresses. The prototype Deltic would soon be on the scene, the forerunner of the class of 22 which would ultimately replace the famous Gresley A4s on the east coast route.

But all of this was of little concern to the multitude of spotters; they were, after all, just prototypes - the 'Britannias' were still 'running in', Southern Region pacifics were being rebuilt, a new Class 8P pacific prototype was ready for trials.The country had an abundance of coal reserves, whilst oil still had to be imported. Taking all these factors into account, British Railways' analysts and planners produced differing forecasts as to the future of steam traction; forecasts which varied immensely, some even predicting steam would last not only to the end of the century but even beyond. Steam was definitely here to stay for some time to come - or was it?

In 1963, the most radical changes since nationalisation were announced under the 'Beeching modernisation scheme', sending shock waves through the entire railway system. In the following few short years, steam locomotives would be withdrawn in their thousands. Building of new steam locomotives would be terminated immediately. Stations on branch lines and main lines alike closed. Main line running sheds - King's Cross, Camden, Nine Elms, Old Oak Common which housed the most famous locomotives in the world would very soon disappear.

The end of a glorious period was fast approaching and the sudden realisation generated a resurgence of interest not only amongst the established rail enthusiasts but throughout the general public, which increased in intensity towards the final 'deadline' of August 1968, the official end to steam traction on British Railways.

This publication covers the period 1961 to 1967, the years when the pacific locomotives were being withdrawn and broken up whilst those still in service were relegated from the premier main line expresses to lesser duties. The author, like many of his contemporaries, suddenly woke up to the reality that the British pacific would very soon be erased from the railway scene and made a final effort to seek out and record photographically remaining examples of these magnificent machines.

60130
56C
A-1

The Delights of Leeds

Any young trainspotter living within affordable distance of Leeds during the 1950s was indeed fortunate. The rich variety of locomotive types which could be seen during a summer Saturday at the two stations, City and Central was a true delight and if access could be gained, either legitimately or otherwise to the three main sheds at Holbeck, Copley Hill or Neville Hill it was an added bonus.

The only slight problem was finding a location from where train movements to both stations could be observed. It wasn't until 1969 that the two stations were redeveloped and combined and one can only fantasise about the trainspotters paradise this would have been had this redevelopment taken place twenty years earlier.

Pacifics in and around Leeds were plentiful; the majority running into Central station from King's Cross and other points along the east coast main line. Indeed many named trains could be seen here; 'The West Riding ', 'The Yorkshire Pullman', 'The White Rose', 'The Queen of Scots Pullman', all of which would more often than not be hauled by a pacific locomotive, many of which were allocated to Copley Hill.

Neville Hill's small stud of A3s could be seen working out of City station on 'The North Briton' and trans-pennine trains.

During the period covered by this book, although the principal services had been given over to the Deltics and Type 4 diesel electrics, steam workings between Leeds and King's Cross did continue up to the closure of Top Shed. Meanwhile, Holbeck at this time acquired a small allocation of A3s which could be seen working 'The Thames-Clyde Express' and 'The Waverley' amongst other trains over the Leeds - Carlisle section. 'Britannias' were also active in a variety of duties out of Leeds. Allocated to Holbeck and Carlisle Kingmoor, they too were regularly seen over the former Midland line between the two cities.

LEEDS CENTRAL STATION **Above** - An immaculate Class A1 from Copley Hill depot No. 60130 *Kestrel* waits the right-away with an afternoon train for King's Cross. Sept '63.

Right - Another A1 Class No. 60149 *Amadis* returns to Copley Hill after bringing in a train of empty stock. Sept '63.

Overleaf - A4 Class 60034 *Lord Faringdon* blasts away from Leeds Central with a London bound express. June '63.

60149

60021

60107
LEEDS
CENTRAL

Previous Page (left) - A4 Class 60021 *Wild Swan* coasts into Leeds Central with a mid-day arrival from London. June '63.

Previous Page (right) - Class A3 No. 60107 *Royal Lancer* receives last minute attention from its crew prior to departure from Leeds Central. June '63.

Below and Opposite - A1 Class 60125 *Scottish Union* awaits the right-away at the signal gantry with an afternoon train for Doncaster. Sept '63.

SCOTTISH UNION

ARRIVALS and DEPARTURES

Above - A3 Class 60063 *Isinglass* snakes through the cross-overs into Leeds Central with the down 'White Rose'. June '63.

Opposite Page (top) - A4 Class 60013 *Dominion of New Zealand* departs Leeds Central with a morning train for King's Cross. Nov '61.

Opposite Page (bottom) - Class A3 60061 *Pretty Polly* at the head of a morning train for Doncaster. Feb '62

60061

60074
THE
AMES-CLYDE
XPRESS

Opposite Page - The crew of Neville Hill A3 60074 *Harvester* chats to a group of young spotters at Leeds City station prior to departure with the second stage of the down 'Thames-Clyde Express'. Nov '61.

Below - Another A3 60080 *Dick Turpin* carrying a Neville Hill shedplate waits at Holbeck depot after bringing in an excursion train from Carlisle. July '63.

Overleaf - 'Britannia Class' 70053 formerly *Moray Firth* awaits departure from Leeds City with a Saturday summer relief down 'Thames-Clyde Express'. March '67.

1S37

12

70025

Northward to Carlisle

In the post war heyday of steam, Carlisle was, unfortunately, well outside the affordable distance from home for anything like regular spotting trips in spite of it being one of the north's most important railway centres. Citadel station was an enviable trainspotter's paradise with its wonderful mix of traffic from every direction - Edinburgh, Glasgow, London and the west midlands, Leeds, Newcastle. Almost every type of ex LMS & LNER locomotive could be seen there; the cream of British Railways' motive power stock; Stanier pacifics on the premier Anglo-Scottish expresses; Gresley, Thompson and Peppercorn pacifics over the Waverley route.

Then came modernisation and the rapid transition from steam to diesel electric and finally electrification of the west coast main line in the 1962-4 period which virtually eliminated steam activity over these routes.

By the end of 1963 the 'Princess Royal' Class was extinct, and the 'Princess Coronation' Class engines were fast disappearing. 'Britannias' were the last of the pacifics to survive and several could be observed still active, working out of Carlisle, mainly over the former Midland line covering a variety of duties from mixed freight to coal and passenger trains. The principal passenger trains using this route, 'The Thames-Clyde Express', 'The Waverley', and the Sheffield-Glasgow could still be seen with a 'Britannia' or a Class A3 in charge on the Leeds-Carlisle section. It also became a not uncommon site in these fast changing times to see Haymarket pacifics working the up 'Waverley' from Edinburgh as far south as Leeds, their former principal duties having been taken over by the Deltics and Type 4s. However, this situation was shortlived as the 'Waverley' route between Carlisle and Edinburgh, in spite of fierce opposition, became another casualty of the Beeching axe and the Midland lost one of its two premier Anglo-Scottish expresses.

Of the three main sheds at Carlisle; Kingmoor, Upperby and Canal, only Kingmoor remained an active steam depot up to its closure in 1967 when it housed all of the remaining Britannias along with a substantial allocation of Stanier Class 5s, 8Fs, and B.R. Standard Class 9Fs, up to their final demise.

'Britannia' Class 70044 *Earl Haig* roars past Keighley South signal box with the down 'Waverley', shortly before the service was withdrawn. Nov '61.

A train of mineral wagons trundles through Skipton station with Stockport (Edgeley) 'Britannia' 70021 formerly *Morning Star* in charge. June '67.

Carlisle (Kingmoor) 'Britannia' 70034 formerly *Thomas Hardy* being turned at Skipton shed ready for its return journey north. May '67.

Blea Moor - 'Britannia' Class 70004 formerly *William Shakespeare* eases out of the loop to continue its journey north with a train of coal wagons after replenishing its tender. June '67.

Previous Page - Ribblehead - 'Britannia' Class 70021 *Morning Star,* miniaturised by the massive structure of the viaduct, makes light work of a short freight train as it nears the end of the climb to Blea Moor with steam to spare. April '67.

Above - Blea Moor - 'Britannia' 70049 formerly *Solway Firth* with the cylinder cocks opened in an attempt to clear a stray sheep from the line ahead, eases southward with a train of empty coal wagons. July '67.

Blea Moor - Another 'Britannia' 70024 formerly *Vulcan* passes the up sidings with a southbound parcels train while a Stanier Class 5 waters up in the loop. April '67.

Overleaf - 'Britannia' Class 70049 formerly *Solway Firth* climbs the final stretch to Ais Gill summit with a train of empty coal wagon, and pulls into the loop, still with a full head of steam, to allow the passage of the up 'Thames-Clyde Express'. July '67.

1M 91
70049

Carlisle (Kingmoor) - The last major operational depot for the remaining ‘Britannias’, sadly no longer carrying their nameplates.

Above - 70024 and 70025, formerly *Vulcan* and *Western Star*, are ready for their next turns south over the Settle-Carlisle route. May ’67.

Opposite Page - 70051, formerly *Firth of Forth*, temporarily resting. July ’67.

70051

70021
46226

Opposite Page (top) - Steam activity still very much in evidence at Kingmoor with an assortment of 'Britannias' and Class 9Fs including 70021, 70028, 92110, 92208 and 70022. Sept '67.

Opposite Page (bottom) - One of the last remaining 'Coronation' Class locomotives 46226 *Duchess of Norfolk*, still working passenger traffic out of Carlisle. Oct '63.

Above - Another 'Coronation' pacific 46254 *City of Stoke-on-Trent* sets out from Citadel station with a train for Birmingham. June '62.

Above - The 'Clans' had a remarkably short life and were among the first B.R. Standard Class locomotives to be withdrawn. Here one of the last survivors, 72001 *Clan Cameron* hurries its train south on the west coast main line at Hest Bank. July '63.

Opposite Page (top) - Under the wires at Crewe. 'Coronation' pacific 46250 *City of Lichfield* ends its journey from Carlisle. April '64.

Opposite Page (bottom) - The same location for 'Britannia' 70048 *The Territorial Army 1908-1958.* April '64.

CITY OF LICHFIELD
46250
THE TERRITORIAL ARMY
1908–1958

Splendour of York

The sight of York station and its famous roof arches must be one of the most familiar in Britain, having appeared in countless railway publications ever since its construction.

For geographic and economic reasons, York was one of the favourite destinations from home base. After the first leg of the journey to Leeds it was often a toss of a coin to decide whether to proceed to Doncaster or to York. Either destination promised an excellent day's spotting, particularly for LNER enthusiasts.

In the period covered by this book, however, although York was still one of the major centres where pacifics could be observed, the station itself had little to offer, especially after the closure of Top Shed in June 1963 when steam operation from King's Cross ended, since diesel electrics had displaced steam from almost all of the east coast main line passenger trains.

On a typical summer day in the early 60s, the first sighting of a pacific at York would often be from the Leeds train as it approached the station; a Class A1 or an A4 simmering on stand-by outside the small south shed. But the priority on arrival was a visit to the main depot at Leeman Road, now the site of The National Railway Museum, where a splendid display of locomotives could be guaranteed.

Legitimate access to the depot was often possible depending on the shed staff on duty at the time and entry to the roundhouse was a delight. Once inside, one could witness an abundance of locomotive types under the diffused lighting filtering through the smoky atmosphere. An A4, A1s, V2s and K3's were a typical variety clustered round the turntable ready for their next calls of duty. The time could well have been a decade and more earlier, so little of this image would have changed.

Outside in the yard, although diesels were more in evidence, plenty of steam activity could still be observed; another A4, this one from Gateshead depot, two more A1s, a number of V2s, amongst them York's own 60847 *St. Peter's School, York A.D.627*, a couple of 'Britannias' and B.R. Standard 9Fs, all in steam preparing for their next turns.

Above - York's own A1 Class 60140 *Balmoral* undergoes a wash and brush-up from the roundhouse crew. Oct '63.

Opposite - Sister engine 60124 *Kenilworth* rests in the sunlight and shadow of the roundhouse. Sept '64.

Another A1 Class 60145 *Saint Mungo* rests in the roundhouse. Sept ’64.

Three pacifics undergoing service in the repair shop at York; A3 Class 60062 *Minoru*, Class A1 60124 *Kenilworth* and an unidentified A3. Oct '63.

Among the engines clustered round the turntable are A4 60029 *Woodcock* and A1 60126 *Sir Vincent Raven.* Oct '63

bove - Another A4, in steam and ready for turning, 60026 *Miles Beevor.* Oct '63.

verleaf Left - Out in the yard, a visiting Gateshead A4 60001 *Sir Ronald Matthews*, stands alongside York's own 2 Class 60847 *St. Peter's School, York A.D.627.* Oct '63.

verleaf Right - Locomotives take their turns at the coaling tower, among them, 'Britannia' Class 70011 *Hotspur.* May '63.

60847
SIR RONALD MATTHEWS

70011

HOTSPUR
70011

Opposite Page - *Hotspur's* formidable front end ready for business. May '63.

Above - A1 Class 60154 *Bon Accord*, coaled, watered and stoked up ready for its next turn. Oct '63.

Overleaf Left - Admiring young spotters look on as A4 Class 60006 *Sir Ralph Wedgwood* takes on more water at York station after bringing in a London bound train from Newcastle. June '63.

Overleaf Right - Class A1 60146 *Peregrine* and A4 60010 *Dominion of Canada* on stand-by at York's south shed. Oct '63.

60006
A-4

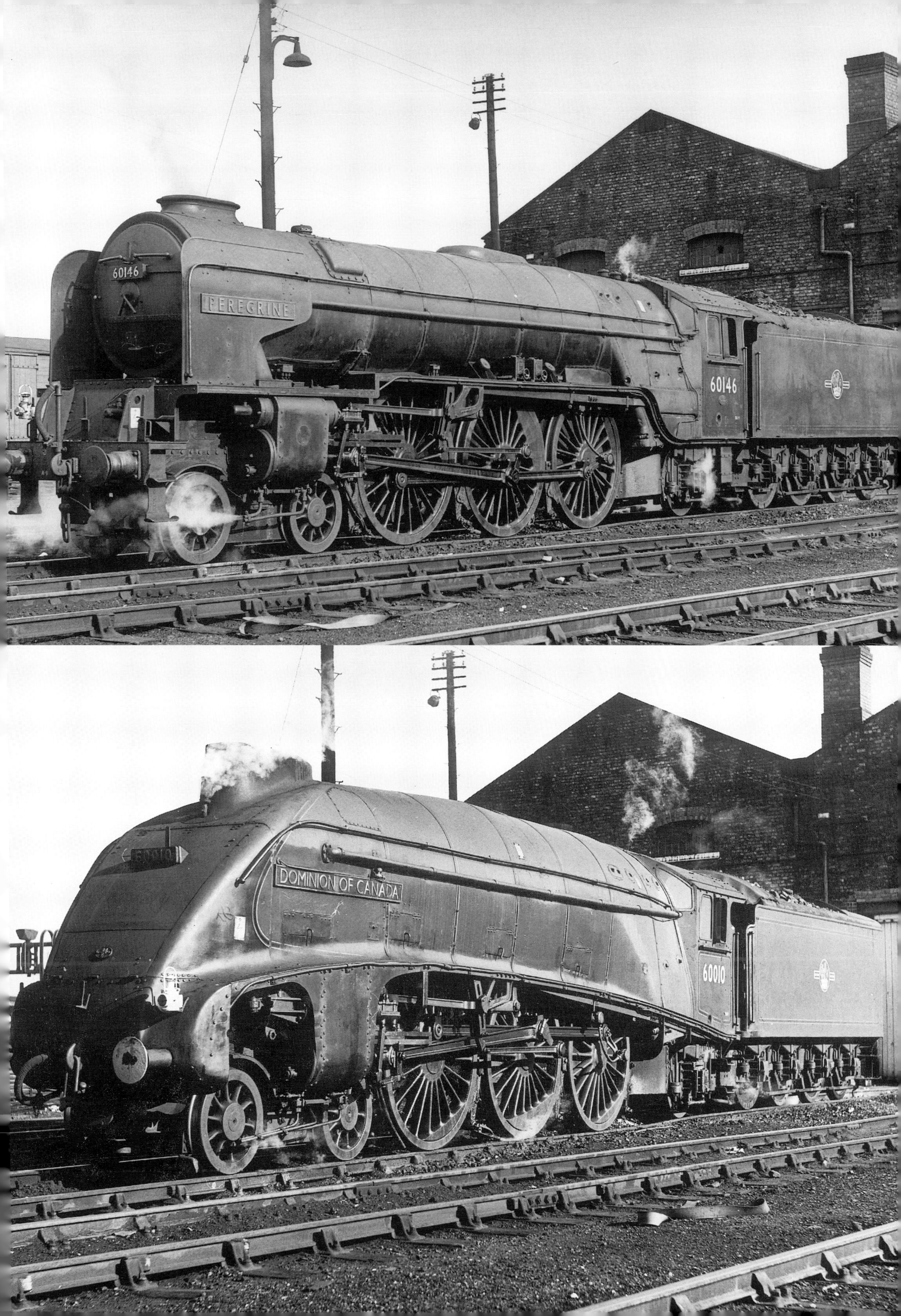
60146
PEREGRINE
60146
DOMINION OF CANADA
60010

Above - Class A1 60141 *Abbotsford* takes the freight avoiding line as it nears York station. April '64.

Opposite Page (top) - The same engine back at York depot.

Opposite Page (bottom) - Sister engine 60121 *Silurian* moves to the water column to replenish its tender. Oct '63.

ABBOTSFORD
60121
SILURIAN
60121

60513
DANTE
526
523
169
60524
HERRINGBONE
523

Opposite Page (top) - One of the last remaining A2/3 Class locomotives 60513 *Dante* takes a southbound freight through York station. Nov '61.

Opposite Page (bottom) - A sister engine in a grimy and neglected condition, 60524 *Herringbone* takes an empty stock train on the same road. Nov '61.

Above - Class A1 60128 *Bongrace* coasts into York station with a southbound train from Newcastle. June '63.

SIR RALPH WEDGWOOD

Doncaster Days

Always a popular venue amongst the northern fraternity of spotters, Doncaster had a certain air of superiority borne of its heritage as the home of the Great Northern Railway Works, builders of some of the world's most famous locomotives - 'Flying Scotsman' and 'Mallard' being the two prime examples. A wealth of locomotive types could always have been seen there on a pre 1960s summer Saturday, the cream of which were the Gresley, Thompson and Peppercorn pacifics hauling the east coast main line expresses.

Train spotting from the station platforms was normally tolerated providing that good behaviour was maintained. Apart from the locals a regular inflow of spotters alighted from their respective trains in the early morning and gathered at the south end of platforms 4 and 5 complete with note books, Ian Allan ABCs, and school satchels of egg sandwiches and bottles of Tizer to set them up for the day.

Doncaster shed and the locomotive works, popularly known as 'The Plant', were very desirable places to gain entry but security was strict and a successful 'sneak-in' to either installation was a rare bonus to a day at Doncaster.

The most popular sightings by far were the A4s. During this period, Haymarket engines, which were rarely seen south of Newcastle, would often be allocated to 'The Elizabethan' which ran non-stop between the capitals. It was therefore quite possible for the locals to spot all thirty four of the class from Doncaster station over a school summer holiday period. Those who did would return to school with self satisfaction bordering on 'cockiness' as they grasped every opportunity to display the first page of locomotive lists in the eastern region stock book to show a 'run' of thirty four underlined numbers.

However, during the 60s the situation changed radically. The Deltics and Type 4s replaced steam on most of the principal main line trains but pacifics were still rostered to lesser duties.

A typical day at this time spent on Doncaster station, up to the closure of Top Shed and the end of steam working from King's Cross, would still reap a worthwhile crop of pacifics. A1s, A3s and A4s were working some of the less prestigious passenger trains between London, Leeds and Newcastle. 'Britannias' in charge of freight trains between the eastern counties and the northern industrial areas passed through Doncaster throughout the day.

Sadly, also at this period, the occasional 'dead' locomotive would be observed being towed into the works on its final journey, ending its glittering career at the plant where it began life some thirty odd years earlier.

Above - A4 60026 *Miles Beevor* sets out for King's Cross with a train from Newcastle. June '63.

Opposite Page - The sharp ends of two more of the class bound for London; 60003 *Andrew K. McCosh* and 60006 *Sir Ralph Wedgwood.* Nov '62.

ANDREW K. McCOSH
SIR RALPH WEDGWOOD

Above - A4 Class 60029 *Woodcock* waits in the bay platform to take on its next train south. Nov '62.

Opposite Page (top) - Class A3 60043 *Brown Jack* sets out from Doncaster with a Leeds-King's Cross train. Nov '62

Opposite Page (bottom) - A1 Class 60117 *Bois Roussel* heads for the depot after uncoupling its train from Leeds. Oct '61.

60043

60117
BOIS ROUSSEL
60117

60063
60063
60110

Opposite Page (top) - A3 Class 60063 *Isinglass* arrives at Doncaster with a Leeds-London train. Oct '62.

Opposite Page (bottom) - Another A3 60110 *Robert the Devil* speeds through Doncaster with a London bound train from Newcastle. Oct '62.

Above - An A1's front end; 60117 *Bois Roussel* in transit from Leeds. Nov '61.

MALLARD
60022
60022
MALLARD
60022
E13032

A typical roster at this period for 60022 *Mallard* - June '62.

Opposite Page (top) - *Mallard* brings the down King's Cross-Hull train into Doncaster.

Opposite Page (bottom) - Detached from the train, *Mallard* reverses to the depot for turning and watering.

Above - On return to the station, *Mallard* waits in the bay platform to take on its next train back to London.

Top - Recoupled to its next train, *Mallard* waits the right-away while an admiring group of youngsters look on.

Bottom - *Mallard* departs Doncaster with its London bound passengers.

Top - A wet Saturday morning as A4 60023 *Golden Eagle* pulls away from platform 4 with a Leeds-King's Cross train. Nov '61.

Bottom - A4 60028 *Walter K. Whigham* with a freshly stoked firebox hustles its London bound train through Doncaster. Nov '61.

60141
ABBOTSFORD

60126
SIR VINCENT RAVEN

Above - A3 Class 60110 *Robert the Devil* sets out from Doncaster with the up 'Yorkshire Pullman'. Oct '62.

Opposite Page (top) - A1 Class 60141 *Abbotsford* speeds through Doncaster with a King's Cross-Newcastle express. Oct '62.

Opposite Page (bottom) - Another A1 60126 *Sir Vincent Raven* heads for the depot after bringing in a train from Leeds. Oct '62.

60134
FOXHUNTER
60134
FOXHUNTER

Opposite Page - A1 Class 60134 *Foxhunter* arrives at Doncaster with a Newcastle-King's Cross train. Nov '61.

Above - Another A1 60145 *Saint Mungo* uncouples from its train. Oct '62.

Overleaf L.H. Page (top) - Almost a capacity crowd of Saturday spotters look on as a pair of 'Britannias', 70034 *Thomas Hardy* and 70011 *Hotspur* double-head a southbound express. Sept '62.

Overleaf L.H. Page (bottom) - Another 'Britannia' Class 70030 *William Wordsworth* trundles through Doncaster with a southbound freight. Sept '62.

Overleaf R.H. Page (top) - An immaculate A3 Class 60059 *Tracery* speeds through Doncaster with a Newcastle-King's Cross train. Sept '62.

Overleaf R.H. Page (bottom) - Class A1 60126 *Sir Vincent Raven* departs Doncaster with a London bound stopping train. Oct '62.

DONCASTER
70034
DONCASTER
70030

60059
F

60126

Two A3 hauled expresses speed past the spotters at the south end of the station - 60066 *Merry Hampton* with a King's Cross-Newcastle train and 60073 *St. Gatien* with a London bound train from Newcastle. Sept '62.

Two more A3s - 60085 *Manna* slows for its Doncaster stop with a King's Cross-Leeds train and 60112 *St. Simon*, with its distinctive 'wing' type smoke deflectors, pulls into Doncaster with a London-Newcastle train. Sept '62.

Top - Class A4 60006 *Sir Ralph Wedgwood* on arrival from Newcastle with a London bound train. Aug '62.

Bottom - Another London bound train pulls away from Doncaster with Class A1 60117 *Bois Roussel* in charge. Nov

op - Class A1 60115 *Meg Merrilies* takes the middle road through Doncaster with a London-Newcastle express. July '62.

ottom - Light engine A3 Class 60047 *Donovan* heads for the depot. July '62.

ROYAL BRITISH HOTEL

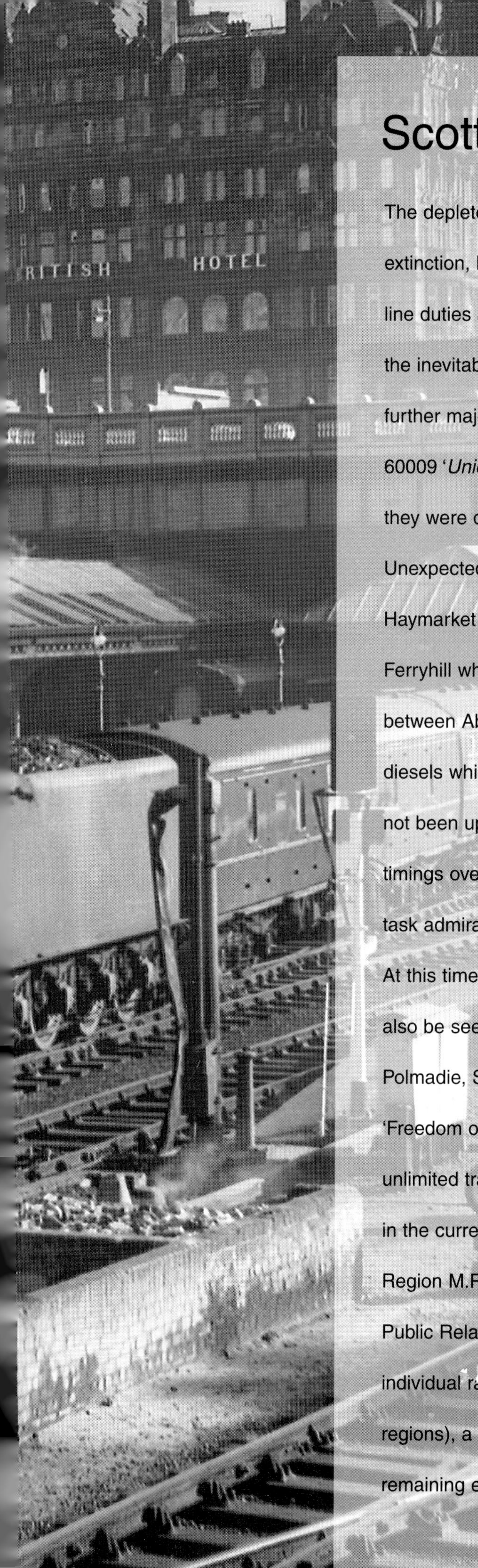

Scottish Swansong

The depleted A4 Class locomotives were by 1964 facing rapid extinction, having been displaced from the premier east coast main line duties and relegated to more menial tasks, beyond which was the inevitable final journey to the breaker's yard. There would be no further major repairs, the general overhaul at Doncaster works of 60009 '*Union of South Africa'* in June 1963 was to be the last, but they were destined not to go out without a final fanfare.

Unexpectedly, a small batch of the remaining A4s, formerly Haymarket and King's Cross engines was transferred to Aberdeen Ferryhill where they were to take over the three-hour expresses between Aberdeen and Glasgow replacing the Brush Type 2 diesels which, much to the delight of A4 enthusiasts, had simply not been up to the job, having failed to maintain the stringent timings over the route. The A4s on the other hand performed the task admirably and ended their days in a blaze of glory.

At this time a scattering of other pacific class locomotives could also be seen over the Scottish region working out of Glasgow Polmadie, St. Margaret's Edinburgh, Dundee Tay Bridge, so with a 'Freedom of Scotland - Silver Ticket' allowing one week's unlimited travel throughout Scotland for the princely sum of £6-6s in the currency of the day, and a shed permit for all the Scottish Region M.P.D.s kindly supplied by British Railways Scottish Region Public Relations Department (always more cooperative towards individual railway enthusiasts than their counterparts in the other regions), a last pursuit was embarked upon to track down these remaining examples of our splendid pacifics.

Above - 'Coronation' Class 46236 *City of Bradford*, one of the fast disappearing types, rests between turns at Glasgow's Polmadie depot. Sept '63.

Opposite Page - Sister engine 46255 *City of Hereford* also waits its next turn at Polmadie. Sept '63.

CITY OF HEREFORD

St. Rollox shed, Glasgow - A4 Class 60011 *Empire of India*, one of the surviving A4s brought in to take over the thre hour expresses between Glasgow (Buchanan Street) and Aberdeen, undergoing preparation for its next trip. Sept '63

Aberdeen (Ferryhill) depot - A2 Class 60532 *Blue Peter* takes a rest between turns on the Aberdeen-Glasgow trips. July '66.

Another of the remaining A4s transferred to Scotland, 60034 *Lord Faringdon* receives attention at Ferryhill depot. July

A former Haymarket A4 60024 *Kingfisher* transferred to Aberdeen (Ferryhill) stands alongside A2 Class 60532 *Blue Peter* outside the shed. July '66.

Overleaf - Front ends of the same two locomotives.

KINGFISHER
D365

BLUE PETER
60532
16T
B91423

WILLIAM WHIT

Opposite Page - Two A4s 'in store' at Ferryhill, 60009 *Union of South Africa*, minus nameplates and tender (which had been earmarked for conversion to an extra water tender for preserved A3 *Flying Scotsman*), and 60004 *William Whitelaw.* July '66.

Above - A4 60024 *Kingfisher* undergoes routine servicing at Ferryhill depot. July '66.

Class A2/3 60524 *Herringbone* almost ready for departure from Aberdeen at the head of its Glasgow bound train. Sep

A2 Class 60532 *Blue Peter* coasts past Ferryhill depot into Aberdeen at the end of its journey from Glasgow. July '66.

Dundee (Tay Bridge) depot - driver's eye view of A2 Class 60530 *Sayajirao* looking towards the bridge. July '66.

A2 Class 60528 *Tudor Minstrel* stands alongside A3 60052 *Prince Palatine* at Dundee (Tay Bridge) depot. Sept ’63.

The driver climbs aboard A2 Class 60530 *Sayajirao* at Dundee (Tay Bridge) depot to take on its next turn of duty. July

A4 Class 60024 *Kingfisher* replenishes its water supply at Perth, midway on its journey with the 'Bon Accord', one of the three hour Aberdeen-Glasgow expresses. July '66.

LORD FARINGDON
60034
60034

Above and Opposite Page - The Perth stop for an immaculate A4 60034 *Lord Faringdon* at the head of 'The Grampian', another of the named Aberdeen-Glasgow trains. July '66.

Haymarket A1 60152 *Holyrood*, relegated to lesser duties, waits at the north end of Edinburgh Waverley to take out a train of empty stock. July '66.

One of the last A2/3 Class engines, 60512 *Steady Aim* at St. Margaret's shed; Edinburgh's remaining active steam depot. Sept '63.

The Bulleids

The innovative features of Oliver Bulleid's pacifics, designed to overcome the stringent weight limits still provoke interesting debate. The unique styling, described as 'air-smoothed' rather than streamlined, the extensive use of welded construction, the continental style wheels and the chain driven valve gear were major new features not previously seen in British pacific locomotives, more surprisingly so since Bulleid had come to the Southern Railway from under the wing of Sir Nigel Gresley yet his designs displayed little LNER influence.
The first major reconstruction of Bulleid's pacifics came in the 1950s following nationalisation when a rebuilding programme began. The air-smoothed casing was removed and replaced with smoke deflectors, the troublesome chain driven valve gear was discarded in favour of the more conventional Walschaerts mechanism. Other features such as the running plate followed the style of the new series of British Railways Standard designs.
Overall the result was a locomotive of splendid appearance of individual style which fortunately also retained the tasteful finishing touch of Bulleid's originals, the nameplates, which themselves were a unique feature. The three classes, 'Merchant Navy', 'Battle of Britain' and the light pacific 'West Country' each carried a nameplate style appropriate to its class.
The Bulleid rebuilding programme, however, was abruptly terminated under Dr. Beeching's radical modernisation scheme but many from all three classes continued to work the main line expresses out of Waterloo well into the 1960s and its home shed, Nine Elms M.P.D. was the last of the principal London depots to end the long tradition of servicing and maintaining main line steam locomotives.
A few days working in London during this period offered the welcome opportunity to enjoy a couple of brief spells at Nine Elms where legitimate access was reasonably easy, and what an experience it turned out to be. A dozen or so active pacifics being watered, coaled, serviced, turned, cleaned or under general repair with many others inside the shed simmering or lying temporarily dormant. This was still very much a 'live' engine shed with all the sounds, smells and general activity that make up the wonderful atmosphere of a major working steam depot. It also proved to be the last time I would ever witness such an installation since within months of my visit, Nine Elms along with its sister sheds at Salisbury, Exmouth and Bournemouth, would be closed and the remaining Bulleid pacifics withdrawn, bringing to an end another phase of the great British steam locomotive story.

Unrebuilt 'Battle of Britain' Class 34086 *219 Squadron* waits at Waterloo to take out a train for Exmouth. May '64.

Rebuilt 'Merchant Navy' Class 35030 *Elder Dempster Lines* waits the right-away with a Bournemouth express. May '64.

34024
825
34024
469
34057

Opposite Page (top) - Rebuilt 'West Country' Class 34024 *Tamar Valley* with time to spare as the crew chat with enthusiasts prior to departure from Waterloo. May '64.

Opposite Page (bottom) - Unrebuilt 'Battle of Britain' Class 34057 *Biggin Hill* reverses out of Waterloo to Nine Elms depot after bringing in a train from Exmouth. May '64.

Above - Rebuilt 'Battle of Britain' Class 34050 *Royal Observer Corps* takes the same short journey back to its home depot at Nine Elms. May '64.

Rebuilt 'West Country' Class 34095 *Brentor*, off duty in Nine Elms yard. May '64.

The neglected run-down state of Nine Elms depot almost at the end of its life is all too evident as another rebuilt 'West Country' Class 34024 *Tamar Valley* receives attention amidst the debris. May '64.

Unrebuilt 'West Country' Class 34019 *Bideford* waits its turn at the coaling plant at Nine Elms. May '64.

Another 'West Country' Class 34001 *Exeter* at the coaling tower in readiness for its next journey from Waterloo. May '64.

Above - Rebuilt 'Merchant Navy' 35013 *Blue Funnel Line* temporarily out of commission at Nine Elms. May '64.

Opposite - Another rebuilt 'Merchant Navy' 35028 *Clan Line* moves to the coaling tower in preparation for its next trip May '64

35028